Happy Father's Day!
Love ya!
Alex
2006

Any man can be a father, but not every man has the loving qualities it takes to be a "dad." It requires a very special man who can put everyone else's needs before his own. Dad, you are one of these men.

— Geri Danks

Blue Mountain Arts®
Bestselling Titles

By Susan Polis Schutz:
To My Daughter, with Love, on the Important Things in Life
To My Son, with Love
I Love You

By Douglas Pagels:
100 Things to Always Remember... and One Thing to Never Forget
For You, Just Because You're Very Special to Me
To the One Person I Consider to Be My Soul Mate

Is It Time to Make a Change?
by Deanna Beisser

To the Love of My Life
by Donna Fargo

A Lifetime of Love ...Poems on the Passages of Life
by Leonard Nimoy

Anthologies:
Always Believe in Yourself and Your Dreams
For You, My Daughter
I Love You, Mom
I'm Glad You Are My Sister
Marriage Is a Promise of Love
May You Always Have an Angel by Your Side
Take Each Day One Step at a Time
Teaching and Learning Are Lifelong Journeys
There Is Greatness Within You, My Son
Think Positive Thoughts Every Day
To My Child
With God by Your Side ...You Never Have to Be Alone

From Your Daughter to You,

DAD,

with So Much Love

A Blue Mountain Arts® Collection
Celebrating the Special Bond
a Father and Daughter Share

Edited by Diane Mastromarino

Blue Mountain Press™

Boulder, Colorado

Library of Congress Control Number: 2003115206
ISBN: 0-88396-798-7

ACKNOWLEDGMENTS appear on page 64.

Certain trademarks are used under license.
BLUE MOUNTAIN PRESS is registered in U.S. Patent and Trademark Office.

Manufactured in China.
First Printing: 2004

 This book is printed on recycled paper.

This book is printed on fine quality, laid embossed, 80 lb. paper. This paper has been specially produced to be acid free (neutral pH) and contains no groundwood or unbleached pulp. It conforms with all the requirements of the American National Standards Institute, Inc., so as to ensure that this book will last and be enjoyed by future generations.

Blue Mountain Arts, Inc.
P.O. Box 4549, Boulder, Colorado 80306

Contents

The Story of a Dad
and His Daughter

A baby girl is born. Simultaneously, from amid the ranks of ordinary men, there emerges a mightily courageous, gallant man — who is quaking in his shoes.

As they grow together, the girl comes to know that her dad is no ordinary man. He can hear the sound of the sun pushing the clouds out of her world, and he helps her to hear it, too. He can taste the worst cookies that she will make, and then eat three or four more from the same batch. He can touch the stars and pull them a little closer to her. He can see the fire of youthful puppy love burning in her heart.

No, this is no ordinary man. He has a body to shield his daughter from strangers, big dogs, and noisy things; a broad expanse of chest to nestle against; and an arm to pillow her head while watching television. He has two strong arms to hold her up to touch the sky, to see inside a bird's nest, or to fly like an airplane.

In her teenage years, he teaches her to respect herself and others. He is always proud of her for trying new things; she doesn't always have to win. He is a wealth of truth in the midst of peer group untruths, an impatient driving instructor, and a light in the window at twelve o'clock on a Friday night. He is the firm cornerstone of the family who gives her values to believe in, a heritage she feels worthy of, and an urgency for living her life completely.

In her adulthood, he could choose to slow down a bit, but he won't. He will still utilize his many resources to teach his daughter well, and somehow his mere presence will continue to trigger the potential in her.

So what does a daughter say to this man of subtle sensitivities and infinite wisdom? She says this...

"I Love You, Dad"

— Elaine C. Frantz

Dad, I Always Want You to Know How Grateful I Am for You

Sometimes in our
fast-paced days
so many things go unsaid
and so many people
get taken for granted.
I don't want that to happen with us, Dad.
You are such an important
person in my life —
one of the few people
who cares so much
and expects so little in return.
I have always felt like
I can count on you for anything
and that I would never be let down.
You go out of your way
to make my life happier
and the little things you do
mean so very much to me.
You have such a big heart
filled with so much kindness and love.
I feel so very lucky to be your daughter.
I want to say thank you —
for all that you do
for all that you are
and for how wonderful my life is...
because you are a part of it.

— Elle Mastro

It's Hard to Find
the Perfect Words

How do you thank someone who has given you the moon and the stars? How do you explain the deepest feelings of the heart? What could a daughter say when the words don't even begin to convey the gratitude? With so much to express, where do you start?

I could spend a lifetime searching for the rights words to say to you. The perfect words would be filled with appreciation for someone who took me by the hand when I was little and who guided me on a pathway toward more happiness than most people will ever know.

The right words would tell you how dear you will always be to me for holding the ladders that reached to my own little stars, for catching me whenever I fell, and for always being there with encouragement, support, and understanding.

Maybe I'll never be able to find those perfect words, but that won't keep me from trying. All my life through, I'll try to express that sweet thanks with each little reminder, and every big hug —

    because you give my heart so much joy
        and you give my life so much love.

— Laurel Atherton

Your Love Is
a Wonderful Gift

All my life you have surrounded me
with a complete and unwavering love.
No matter how far I've strayed or
how many disagreements have come
between us, I never questioned the
love you have for me... it was always
there providing me with support,
guidance, and stability. I cannot thank
you enough for offering your heart to
me without ever asking for anything
in return.

Knowing that your love surrounds me
has always given me the courage to
follow my dreams and the confidence
to find my independence. I know there
were times when I hurt you and times
when I made decisions you may not
have agreed with, but through it all,
I have always known your love was
unconditional, and that knowledge
is the most incredible gift I could
ever receive.

— Elle Mastro

I Am So Thankful that
I Have a Father like You

The very best measure of success for any
man is not to be charted by the work
he has done in the world, but by the
accomplishments he has made as a father.
The greatest men are not those who try
to go down in history books; they're
those who try to raise their children in
the most special surroundings of all.

Dad, thank you for helping to raise me in
an environment of caring, encouragement,
and love. Your influence on my life is
woven into the colors and the texture of
so much of what my world is today —
from the times you held me, the stories
you told me, the hugs you gave me, the
tears you dried, the laughter you inspired,
and the wisdom you have shared. All
these things have helped me to survive.
And sometimes... even to succeed!

To this very day, I still find myself leaning on you, learning from you, and wishing I could find a way to express all my love and gratitude.

I seek out the wisdom you have ingrained within me. You are with me so often. I listen for that spirit, that sense, that sure-footed way of walking along life's paths.

And it's still the case that I may stumble sometimes, but I learned a long time ago... the more I keep you with me, the less I fall... and the more joy I know.

I'm so glad that I have a father like you. I think you're the greatest!

— R. L. Keith

One Thing Will
Never Change

Life is so unpredictable. Changes always come along… in big ways and small steps, sometimes giving us a little nudge and other times turning our whole world upside down. So many changes; some subtle and almost unnoticeable, some drastic and more difficult to deal with.

But throughout all of life's changing and rearranging, I'm so glad that there is one wonderful thing that will never change.

In the passing of life's moments, I know that yesterday is already gone and that tomorrow will soon be here. The one thing I will take with me in all the days that lie ahead… is the one thing that has seen me through so many times in the past. It's something that will never change.

You are such a steady, strong, and beautiful part of my life. You never cease to amaze me with the constancy of your giving, the unselfishness of your heart, and the reassurance of your smile.

And I want you to know that my special feelings for you are going to last
　　　forever and ever and ever.

— Marta Best

I'll Always Be
Your Little Girl

Even though I'm grown up now,
I really don't mind if you still
    consider me your "little girl,"
because you do protect me now
    as you did years ago —
you just disguise it in different ways.

Instead of giving me your hand to hold
    as you did long ago,
today you give me wisdom
    so I don't go astray.

And instead of calling out my name
    and expecting an answer,
now you call me on the phone
    just to say you're thinking of me.

You don't give me toys
    to play with anymore;
instead, you give me
    the treasure of your time
        that reaches beyond the moment.

But some things between fathers and
    daughters don't change no matter
        how many years pass —
the warm hugs, the certainty
of laughter when we're together,
the simple security in knowing you're there,
and that unshakable feeling that your love
    will always be with me.

No matter how old I am,
I like the idea that I'll never outgrow
    my need for you, my dad.

— Barbara Vecqueray

To My Role Model,
My Dad

I have come across so many people who have grown up without good role models in their lives. I feel so lucky to have you as my father. Having such a strong, positive person to look up to and model my life after has helped me to become the person I am today. You have built the steppingstones for me to become the best person I can be.

With your guidance and your friendship, I have always felt so safe and secure, and I have had the confidence to set goals and meet them without apprehension. You have always believed in me and in my dreams, and because of that I know I will always have the courage and strength to keep on believing in myself. You have been the greatest father I ever could have asked for.

— Deana Marino

You Are Not Only My Father...
You Are My Friend

— ❧ —

Friendship is opening up to one another.
Sharing thoughts and feelings in a way that
never felt very comfortable before. It is a
complete trust, sweetened with a lot more
understanding and communication than many
people will ever know. Friendship is a gift,
continually giving happiness. It is strong and
supportive, and few things in all the world
will ever compare with the joy that comes
from its wonderful bond.

— Mia Evans

It is the comfort, the security, the knowing that with
you in this world I never have to feel alone. It is your
belief in me, the uplifting words, the genuine advice
that moves me through life. It is the kindness of your
heart, the gift of yourself, the hands outstretched
to pick me up when I fall. It is these things that make
you more than my father. It is these things that make
you my greatest friend.

— Deana Marino

I have been blessed in having the best dad in the whole world. You have always been there when I needed you, and believe me, I've needed you a lot.

I'm so glad that you're someone I can go to when I need to talk things over. You always have a way of making everything look brighter, every obstacle look surmountable, and every problem look solvable. You have an answer for everything.

I am lucky to have been blessed with a very loving and supportive family. But you, Dad, are my best friend, my biggest supporter, my pillar of strength, and the person I look up to more than anybody else in this whole world.

— Kellie Dann

Being Your Daughter
Is a Wonderful Gift

We can't have everything
    in life.
There will always be things
that we wish had been
    different...

But amidst life's imperfections
are those rare and special gifts
that we would never change —
the perfect ones that could
only have come from
    heaven itself.

Those gifts bring
immeasurable joy
to our hearts, our souls,
    and our lives —
like the gift of being
    your daughter.

— Lynn Barnhart

What a Little Girl Is to Her Dad

Little girls are the nicest things that happen to people. They are born with a little bit of angel-shine about them, and though it wears thin sometimes, there is always enough left to lasso your heart — even when they are sitting in the mud, or crying temperamental tears, or parading up the street in Mother's best clothes.

A little girl can be sweeter (or badder) more often than anyone else in the world. She can jitter around, and stomp, and make funny noises that frazzle your nerves, yet just when you open your mouth, she stands there demure with that special look in her eyes. A girl is Innocence playing in the mud, Beauty standing on its head, and Motherhood dragging a doll by the foot.

God borrows from many creatures to make a little girl. He uses the song of a bird, the squeal of a pig, the stubbornness of a mule, the antics of a monkey, the spryness of a grasshopper, the curiosity of a cat, the speed of a gazelle, the slyness of a fox, the softness of a kitten, and to top it all off He adds the mysterious mind of a woman.

A little girl likes new shoes, party dresses, small animals, first grade, noisemakers, the girl next door, dolls, make-believe, dancing lessons, ice cream, kitchens, coloring books, make-up, cans of water, going visiting, tea parties, and one boy. She doesn't care so much for visitors, boys in general, large dogs, hand-me-downs, straight chairs, vegetables, snowsuits, or staying in the front yard. She is loudest when you are thinking, prettiest when she has provoked you, busiest at bedtime, quietest when you want to show her off, and most flirtatious when she absolutely must not get the best of you again.

Who else can cause you more grief, joy, irritation, satisfaction, embarrassment, and genuine delight? She can muss up your home, your hair, and your dignity — spend your money, your time, and your patience — and just when your temper is ready to crack, her sunshine peeks through and you've lost again.

Yes, she is a nerve-racking nuisance, just a noisy bundle of mischief. But when your dreams tumble down and the world is a mess — when it seems you are pretty much a fool after all — she can make you a king when she climbs on your knee and whispers, "I love you best of all!"

— Alan Beck

Daddy, I Remember

Daddy, I remember not so long ago,
days when I was but a shadow
towered by a man as strong as Superman
who could cradle me with one arm
and carry me up the mountain of stairs.

Daddy, I remember many anxious afternoons,
wearing out those old front porch steps
and waiting for the man in a suit
to come walking down the sidewalk
　　with a kind, familiar face.
I remember tearing through our front yard,
yelling out your title, tackling your legs as
you lifted me up with an affectionate hug.

Daddy, I remember Saturday afternoons
when you would take me into town,
where, with the quarter you gave me,
I could buy a month's worth of candy and
comic books to last me through the week.

Daddy, I remember many sleepless nights
when nightmares had me believing that
there were snakes on my pillow,
spiders on the walls,
and a pack of wolves on my heels.
To your room I fled,
for I knew those things did not exist there.
Instead, there was a brave, strong arm
to hold me close and tell me
"everything is all right."

Daddy, I remember the wall I built
    around us
when you were the only man in my life.
When others approached,
up into your arms I leapt,
knowing I would be safe and sound
and could shield myself behind your neck.

Daddy, most of all, I remember
the love and understanding you always showed,
the naps we took, the games we played,
and all the time you gave me.
Daddy, you are still my best friend,
and those old memories are still alive
within my heart and mind.

— Cynthia H. Delgado

A Father's Love

There is something ultimate in a father's love, something that cannot fail, something to be believed against the whole world.

— Frederick W. Faber

A father's love is at once the most tender and powerful force you'll ever know. It remains in your heart forever and is there whenever you need encouragement, warmth, or comfort.

— Jane Andrews

From you, Dad, I've learned
that love is kind
   and accepting
that it is comforting
   and attentive

From you I've learned
that love is unconditional
it is patient and understanding
it is open-minded
   and open-hearted

From you I've learned
that love is encouraging
it cheers you on
and gives you hope
it consoles your heart
   and holds your hand

From you I've learned
that love is the greatest gift
someone can give
   and I thank you
for sharing that gift
   with me

— Elle Mastro

Why a Daughter
Wants to Be
like Her Dad

I want to be the greatest teacher
   of forgiveness;
I want to offer love from my heart.
I want to always look for
   the positive.
I want to be full of the love
   that never gives up.
I want to help in practical ways
   to make someone else's life easier.
I want to give a word of encouragement
   each day.
I want to remain hopeful always.
I want to make all my life a prayer.
I want to be a constant friend
   to others from day to day.
I want to have protective, encircling arms
   and love that reaches out.
I want to mirror all the things
   that you've been to me.

— Linda E. Knight

A Father Is So Many Wonderful Things

A father may not know your birthdate, but he can tell you about the best day of his life... the day you were born.

A father isn't the one who buys the birthday and Christmas presents, but he is the one who, for no apparent reason, will take you out for ice cream.

A father is not someone who will give you everything you ask for, but he will make sure you have everything you need.

A father may not always make it home for dinner, but he will always be there when you need him.

A father is not someone who will always like the clothes you choose or the way you do your hair, but he will always think you are beautiful.

A father is someone who is tough on you, but twice as hard on himself.

A father is someone whose arms you can always run to.

A father is someone who gives you his heart the moment you are born. He will always be a part of you and will always love you.

— Cindy Robert

All My Life
You Have Been
There for Me

My childhood days are behind me, but memories linger
in my mind.
I remember so many times made special because you
were always there for me.

I appreciate the way you raised me in a home full of
love and acceptance,
Giving me a sense of direction and values to guide me
in life.

You always know when I need your help, even before
I ask.
You have been my mender of everything, from broken
toys to fallen dreams.

Whenever I have little triumphs that I am anxious to
share with someone,
I always know you will express an excitement that
matches my own.

Your strength and gentleness have always
been very impressive to me —
Your strength supports through times of weakness
and your gentleness is expressed in hugs filled with love.

You have always played a big part in my life, and
I will forever be grateful.

— Karen Richey

Now I Know Why, Dad

Now I know why you're so wonderful. Now that I'm older, I see just as much with my heart as I do with my eyes. Now that I understand things a little more, I'm better at being able to realize the inherent value in your smiles, your words, and in the treasure of every single way you show your love.

Now I know why you're so precious to me. You have believed in me and encouraged me all my life. You are patient and strong. You dry tears and mend hurts, always taking me back to the path that leads to my blessings. You teach me so much and provide for me so well.

Now I know why you're so important to me. You listen to me with your heart and you talk to me with your soul. You are generous and giving, and you have sacrificed in your lifetime to make so many things better in mine.

Now I know why you're so amazing to me.
You do anything and everything any child
could ever ask a father to do, and then —
as if that wasn't enough — your eyes smile
my way and you always seem to say, "Is
there anything I can do for you?"

You know what, Dad? There is something
you can do. You can lovingly remember that
there are so many times when the one thing
that always and forever sees me through is
just knowing... that I have the most
wonderful father in all the world... in you.

— Douglas Pagels

What Is a Dad?

A dad is someone who
wants to catch you before
   you fall
but instead picks you up,
   brushes you off,
and lets you try again.

A dad is someone who
wants to keep you from
   making mistakes'
but instead lets you find
   your own way,
even though his heart breaks
in silence when you get hurt.

A dad is someone who
holds you when you cry,
   scolds you
when you break the rules,
has faith in you even
   when you fail,
and shines with pride
   when you succeed.

— Suzan Ceylise

Dads are angels, cowboys,
    and superheroes.
Dads save the day
and then take out the trash.
Dads are teachers and storytellers
    and magicians.
Dads are Santa Clauses
    and shining stars.
Dads are miracle-makers
and examples and role models.
Dads are artists and cooks and friends.
Dads are everything
    we need them to be...
and sometimes even a little bit more.

— Ashley Rice

You Make Our House a Home

What is a home? A roof to keep out the rain. Four walls to keep out the wind. Floors to keep out the cold. Yes, but home is more than that. It is the laugh of a baby, the song of a mother, the strength of a father. Warmth of living hearts, light from happy eyes, kindness, loyalty, comradeship. Home is first school and first church for young ones, where they learn what is right, what is good, and what is kind. Where they go for comfort when they are hurt or sick. Where joy is shared and sorrows eased. Where fathers and mothers are respected and loved. Where the simplest food is good enough for kings because it is earned. Where money is not so important as loving kindness. Where even the teakettle sings from happiness. That is home.

— Ernestine Schumann-Heink

Home is the place I feel
most myself in
It is my beautiful source
     of comfort
It is the place I go for strength
Home is where I know
there will always be a light on
and that no matter how far I travel
there will be open hearts
     and open arms
welcoming me at the door

— Deana Marino

It's the inside of a house
that makes it a home.
It's not furnishings or décor,
but the family photo albums
filled with loving memories.
Home is the people who gather
at dinnertime,
the cozy atmosphere of talk and laughter,
and the informality of sharing
everything together.
It's the privilege of having
friendship close by
and being loved despite
your faults;
it's the deepest level of understanding,
the highest peak of caring,
and being part of something
so unique.
There's no greater place on earth
than the inside of a house
filled with those who make home
everything it's meant to be.
It's where memories are made
from the warmth of smiles,
spontaneous and caring hugs,
and those who are remembered
with love.
Home is my special memory of you.

— Barbara J. Hall

For All You Do, Dad

For those times I've missed saying
"Thank you," I want to thank you
now for being a soft and gentle light
in my life.

Thank you for the thoughtfulness
you've shown to me so many times.
Thank you for all the things you've
done for me... not out of obligation,
but out of the goodness of your
heart and in the spirit of love and
concern for my happiness and
well-being. You have brought joy and
encouragement to my life, and I want
you to know that I appreciate every
kindness you've shown me.

Thank you for the loyalty and trust
you inspire. Thank you for the
lessons in humanity that I have learned
from you. Thank you for being such a
beautiful example of a caring person.
I know I've said it before, but it is
worthy of repetition... I appreciate you
and I want to thank you once again...
for everything.

— Donna Fargo

What I Would Like
to Give to You

A heartfelt thank-you... for all the things
you do for me.

My assurance... that I really <u>do</u> remember
the things you taught me,
and I always will.

Plenty of reasons... for you to feel proud of me,
which I'll achieve by always
striving to be and do my best.

A sincere apology... for any headaches
I may have caused you
when I was growing up.

A gift certificate... to be redeemed anytime,
as many times as you want,
for anything I can ever do.

My promise... that no matter how far away
from home I may travel,
you are never far from my heart.

My continued commitment... to our family
and the values you have taught me.

Recognition... for all the great things
you've done in your life.
(Not the least of which was me!)

An invitation... to always be a part of my life,
and to never feel that you have to ask.

A bunch of wishes... that you have
the peace, joy, and happiness in your life
that you so deserve.

My love... forever and always.

— Anna Marie Edwards

What It Means
to Have a Father
like You

It means I have someone
who cares enough to
    really listen
and who gives good advice
only when it's asked for...

Having a father like you
means I have someone
who accepts me just
    the way I am.
I have someone who shares
the same wonderful memories
and who has been with me
through some of the hardest
    and best times of my life.

I have someone I can count on
who believes in me
    and encourages me to try.
It means there is a man in this world
who knows me better
than practically anyone else
and thinks I'm pretty special...
    just like he is.

— Barbara Cage

The Gift of a Family

A family is
A place to belong;
A place with
Understanding, support, and trust;
A place where you're appreciated
Just for being you.
A family is
A place where you're loved
Even when you're wrong;
A place where peace abides
Even in the midst of chaos;
A place to talk about what could be
As if it *really* could be;
A place for believing
In people, in yourself,
And in the power
That brought
This family together.
A family is your heart's home —
Wherever you go,
Whatever you do,
And whoever you turn out to be.

A family is
A warm and comfortable place
Forever.

— Barbara J. English

The best feeling in this world
    is family.
From it, we draw love,
    friendship, moral support,
and the fulfillment of every
    special need within our hearts.
In a family, we are connected to
    an ever-present source
of sunny moments, smiles and laughter,
understanding and encouragement,
and hugs that help us grow
    in confidence
    all along life's path.
Wherever we are,
whatever we're doing,
whenever we really need to feel
    especially loved, befriended,
        supported, and cared for
            in the greatest way,
our hearts can turn to the family
and find the very best
    always waiting for us.

— Barbara J. Hall

You Are So
Important to My Life

Dad, in times of weakness
you've shown me
what strength is all about.
You've given me guidance,
reminding me that no one
has all the answers.
You've pointed to the hope
of each new day
and how it provides
an opportunity
to learn and grow.
Your love and support
have carried me through
many painful times of loneliness
and moments that fell short
of my high expectations.
What has been most special to me
is how you've always celebrated
my successes with pride.
I can never repay you enough
for all you've done for me, Dad.
You have helped me to become
the person I am.

— Kelly D. Williams

Forever... You Will Be
a Part of Me

⤜

I wish you could know
how much you have influenced my life.
You have shaped me as a human being,
making me the best I can be inside.
You have taught me wrong from right,
giving me room to experience things on my own.
You have nurtured me,
giving me love in your own special way —
whether it was a hug, a smile, a wink,
or a few quiet words of praise.
You have helped me,
giving me advice
on what you thought was right.

You have supported me by always
being there to help see me through.
You have given me a life
shaped by morals and values
that could only be passed down from you.
You have given me everything,
and by doing so,
I'm not only a part of you —
you've become a part of me.

— Stephanie Spilotro

Dad, what do you see
    when you look at me?
I hope you see some small piece
    of yourself.

All my life, I've been modeling myself after
you, believing that maybe one day,
someone would say, "You remind me of
your father." That would be the highest
compliment. I like to think that who I really
am, on the inside, came from watching you.

Thank you, Dad, for being you.
When I am at my best,
    you are the very best
        part of me.

— Ginger Goslin Martin

You Will Always
Be My Father

Love takes many different forms.
For some people, it means
spending time together
talking, laughing, and
working alongside one another.
For some, it is a hug
or a word of praise.
For others, it is simply
an unspoken understanding that
family is forever;
it is a bond that can never be
broken, no matter where we go
or what we do.
As the years pass,
I become more and more aware
of how important that bond really is,
and although I may rarely say it,
I become more appreciative
of your role in my life.
You are my father, and you
will always be my father.
And because of that,
you will always have a profound
place in my heart.

— Pamela Koehlinger

Wherever I Go...

No matter what I achieve
or how far I travel in this world
No matter how much I learn
or how many people I meet
No matter how the years
pass by so quickly
and life changes before my eyes
there will always be one thing
that remains the same —
You will always be my dad
I will always be your daughter
and you will be a part of me...
    forever.

— Deana Marino

...You Are with Me

When we cannot be together
you are still with me —
your voice guiding my steps
your smile brightening my day
Our memories linger
as a reminder that your love
   is never far
and I feel secure in who I am
and in the decisions I make
because I have you as my father
and I know you will be with me
every step of the way.

— Deana Marino

No matter how many miles
come between us
and how many twists and turns
we make as we travel life's journey,
you will always have
a very special place in my heart —
a place that no one else
   will ever fill.

— Jason Blume

I'm So Proud
to Be Your Daughter

Dad, you are the one who always believed in me. You taught me to see that my life was filled with infinite possibilities. You wiped away the tears that sometimes came my way, and I knew that your caring heart would always be there for me.

I've always been proud of you. The legacy you have given me has been so rich. It's not the material things that have mattered to me, but all the ways you have cared for me that I can't forget.

Whenever problems have threatened me, I've always known that I could come to you for understanding and guidance. In your tender, caring way, you listened with your heart and brought such comfort to me in those troubled days of mine.

Your love has been a priceless gift to me. Your faith in me gave me the courage to pursue my dreams so confidently.

I just want you to know that I will always be "Daddy's girl." Because of your love and faith in me, I have become the woman that I was meant to be. The precious memories that we share will always be a source of strength to me.

I have been so blessed to have you as my dad.

— Diane Rotterman Drescher

Thank You, Dad

Thank you, Dad, for being there when I was a child. Thank you for always hearing me even when the words were inside and I couldn't really say what I was feeling.

Thank you for accepting me even when I was losing or making mistakes, or when I couldn't promise you that I was giving my best.

Thank you for knowing the person inside me — the one who would eventually become the person I am today.

Thank you for encouraging me to always reach out to others, to listen to my inner voice and trust my instincts, to look into my heart and soul and always know that there, I would find my best teacher.

Thank you for believing in me and knowing that I would come through when I was traveling a rocky road and the horizon seemed gray instead of blue.

Thank you for being someone who is patient, wise, and honest; someone who could always find the beauty inside.

Thank you for being someone I am proud and honored to call my dad — the best man I know; the one who has given my life hope.

Thank you for everything... especially for being yourself.

— Regina Hill

ACKNOWLEDGMENTS

We gratefully acknowledge the permission granted by the following authors, publishers, and authors' representatives to reprint poems or excerpts from their publications.

Kellie Dann for "I have been blessed...." Copyright © 2004 by Kellie Dann. All rights reserved.

Lynn Barnhart for "Being Your Daughter Is a Wonderful Gift." Copyright © 2004 by Lynn Barnhart. All rights reserved.

Cynthia H. Delgado for "Daddy, I Remember." Copyright © 2004 by Cynthia H. Delgado. All rights reserved.

Linda E. Knight for "I want to be the greatest teacher...." Copyright © 2004 by Linda E. Knight. All rights reserved.

Cindy Robert for "A Father Is So Many Wonderful Things." Copyright © 2004 by Cindy Robert. All rights reserved.

Barbara J. Hall for "It's the inside of a house...." Copyright © 2004 by Barbara J. Hall. All rights reserved.

PrimaDonna Entertainment Corp. for "For All You Do, Dad" by Donna Fargo. Copyright © 2002 by PrimaDonna Entertainment Corp. All rights reserved.

Barbara Cage for "What It Means to Have a Father like You." Copyright © 2004 by Barbara Cage. All rights reserved.

Barbara J. English for "A family is...." Copyright © 2004 by Barbara J. English. All rights reserved.

Ginger Goslin Martin for "Dad, what do you see...." Copyright © 2004 by Ginger Goslin Martin. All rights reserved.

Jason Blume for "No matter how many miles...." Copyright © 2004 by Jason Blume. All rights reserved.

A careful effort has been made to trace the ownership of selections used in this anthology in order to obtain permission to reprint copyrighted material and give proper credit to the copyright owners. If any error or omission has occurred, it is completely inadvertent, and we would like to make corrections in future editions provided that written notification is made to the publisher:

BLUE MOUNTAIN ARTS, INC., P.O. Box 4549, Boulder, Colorado 80306